Heart of a Champion

Heart of a Champion

The Life and Legacy of Coach Bill Freeman

Jennifer Freeman with Tina Wendling

Heart of a Champion: The Life and Legacy of Coach Bill Freeman by Jennifer Freeman with Tina Wendling
Copyright © 2018 by Jennifer Freeman

Cover and interior design by Margaret Haik

ISBN-13:978-1717577733
ISBN-10:1717577733

Create Space Independent Publishing Platform
North Charleston, South Carolina
Printed in the United States of America

Available at Amazon.com and other book retailers.

*In loving memory
of my beloved father,
without whom,
I would not be the woman I am today.*

Contents

Foreword

I have played a lot of football in my day, and I do mean a lot. At sixty-eight years old, my head is still full of countless plays, drills, and chalkboard X's and O's. Sometimes, the memories of triumphant victories and staggering defeats feel closer and more real than present day. I was blessed—blessed to be able to play the game I loved for as long as I did and blessed by the many people and places that shaped my career and my life. None of those people or places are as near and dear to my heart as Osawatomie High School and the late Bill Freeman.

I will never forget my very first practice with him in the summer of 1965. Mr. Freeman was like no other coach I had ever known, and on that sweltering August day, I thought he was absolutely crazy. He made us run longer and further and condition harder than anything I had ever experienced. He left us all scratching our heads, wondering who in the heck he was and how in the world we were going to survive an entire season.

The truth is, we did survive. In fact, we did more than survive —we thrived, thanks in large part to the tough expectations set by Mr. Freeman. He pushed us hard, but we rose to the challenge. The two years I played for him at Osawatomie High School were exhilarating. The first year, we went 7 and 2, and the second, we were undefeated—the perfect season. That season, among all the others I've played, including fifteen in the nfl, will always be one of my most cherished football memories.

I was that kid. You know, the one who never wanted to come indoors when it got dark, the one who wanted to finish the pick-up game no matter what, the one who wanted to win at everything and who pushed himself harder than anyone else ever could have. That was me, and in Bill Freeman, I met my match. He was a grinder, too—tough and driven. He taught me to be mentally tougher than I ever imagined I could be. We got each other, we respected each other, and I wanted to make him proud.

I played for the Green Bay Packers from 1976 to 1985. Although the legendary Vince Lombardi had already retired by that point, you can imagine the stories I was regaled with on an almost daily basis. He was loved and revered as one of the best coaches of all time. When I heard guys speak of him, I couldn't help but think of Mr. Freeman. The way players described Coach Lombardi and his style sounded so familiar, so akin to the way Bill Freeman approached the game and his players.

Like Lombardi, Freeman walked the talk. He believed in working hard at everything he did, and he instilled that work ethic in his teams. Winning didn't have to be fancy or pretty, either. Bill's approach was simple—four or five plays executed at the highest level of proficiency. He believed in taking what you had and doing the absolute best with it you could. His motto, "You only get something out of it if you put something in," still echoes in my mind after all these years.

I saw Bill after high school, often on the sidelines at K-State where I played college ball. After I was drafted to the NFL, I saw him less frequently, but we visited from time to time when I returned home. What always struck me about those visits was how interested Bill was in my life outside of football. He wanted to know how I was doing, how school was going, and later about my marriage and family. He genuinely cared about his players, not just for the period of time they played for him, but forever afterwards. He was truly one of those beloved coaches and teachers, one who stands out for a lifetime in the hearts and minds of those he coached and taught.

When I think of Bill, I am grateful for having had the opportunity to play for him and even more grateful to have been able to call him my friend later in life. He was truly a rare find, a precious stone like the arrowheads he loved to hunt. He coached and taught hundreds of men and women and showed us how to be winners, both on and off the field of play. His dogged determination and relentless drive for perfection were overshadowed only by his genuine kindness and soft-heartedness. And if there was anything he loved more than coaching football and track, it was, without a doubt, his family. He was a loving and devoted husband, father, and grandfather, and I can think of no one better equipped to share his legacy with the world than his daughter, Jennifer. She has worked hard to preserve the memory and legacy left by her father so that others will know of his impact on Kansas high school sports. More importantly, she has been a tireless advocate for those who, like her father, suffer from Alzheimer's, and by sharing his story, hopes to provide some bit of solace and camaraderie to others losing their loved ones to this horrible disease.

To Bill Freeman—thank you for a lifetime of lessons and love, and to Jennifer, thank you for having the courage and generosity to share your dad's legacy with all of us.

-Lynn Dickey

Bill Freeman, Lynn Dickey, and Jennifer Freeman at Lynn's football themed resturant in Kansas City, circa 1986.

Introduction

The clankity-clank of the muffler on Dad's dilapidated, old Ford truck lumbering up the road unceremoniously announced his arrival home after football practice every evening. That was always my favorite part of the day. Football kept him busy, not just in the fall, but all year round, which is probably why, as I grew older, I found ways to spend time with him as much on the field as off. The boys on the team used to call me "Little Wild Bill, Jr.," which I loved because it made me feel like I belonged there. I would ride the bus with the team, go to their practices, and follow my dad around like his shadow.

We even had our own little ritual on game night. As the coaches ran out on the field, I would walk up to my dad and give him a giant hug. I repeated that ritual every Friday night during football season from my early grade school days until my junior year in high school. I only missed one time, and that was because Halloween fell on a Friday that year. I was terribly torn. Do I go to the game, or do I go trick-or-treating with my friends? I chose the latter, and my dad's team lost that night. Forever afterward he jokingly blamed the loss on me. He said my pre-game hug brought him good luck.

The truth is, my dad didn't need luck because he was one hell of an old school football coach. He ended his career as one of the winningest high school football coaches in Kansas state history, with an overall record of 242-82-3 and eight state championships. A small man himself, he learned to play tough while he was an offensive guard at Emporia State University. At only one hundred, sixty pounds, what he lacked in size, he made up for in aggressiveness and attitude, and that is what he taught his players. He believed in working hard and playing hard, leaving it all out there on the field. He also understood that games are rarely won or lost physically, but rather mentally, so he spent a great deal of time preparing his players mentally for the challenge ahead, and it certainly paid off.

More impressive than his winning record, however, is the number of young men whose lives my dad touched in profound and permanent ways. Many of his players went on to play in college and five even played in the NFL, but when they come back to visit or speak about my dad in interviews, they rarely talk about the wins. What they remember most is how much my dad cared about each and every one of his players, how he inspired them to be their very best, and how he used football to impart life lessons they carry with them to this day.

My dad's former players love him, as do I. He is my hero.

Humble, unassuming, devoted, and tough as nails. Watching him decline and finally slip away from Alzheimer's was the most painful experience of my life. Now that he's gone, his memory lives on in the hearts and minds of all who knew him. Whether it was as a coach, father, husband, friend, or colleague, Bill Freeman made an impact in this world. That is what I want to share—my dad's lasting legacy on and off the field. I truly hope you find the stories in this book uplifting and encouraging. In a world darkened by much division, we can all learn a little something from a Kansas high school football coach who saw the very best in everyone, who believed that everyone should have a fair shot, and who lived his life putting others before himself.

Chapter 1
Man, Husband, and Father

"A winner is someone who recognizes his God-given talents,
works his tail off to develop them into skills, and uses these
skills to accomplish his goals. "
Larry Bird

Born on January 27, 1931 in the little farming town of
Burlington, Kansas, my dad was the second child of Harold and
Erma Freeman. His love of the land and fascination with nature
must have been a seed planted deep when he was a young boy,
running and playing on his parents' farm. Working the land
always calmed him down, helped him center, and energized him
in a way that nothing else could.

I assume his childhood was fairly uneventful, as he never
shared much about it. As an adult, he had a great relationship
with his older sister, Helen, so I imagine them as children

laughing together, sharing adventures, and probably causing some trouble along the way. A natural athlete, it only made sense that after graduating from Burlington High School in 1949, Dad went on to play football at Emporia State University, lettering all four years as an offensive guard. Bill Freeman was not a large man—ever—so to play college ball as an offensive guard was quite an

Bill Freeman, Burlington High School graduation photo, 1949

accomplishment. At five-eight, one hundred, sixty pounds, dwarfed by his opponents, he was the epitome of sheer grit and determination on the line. My dad once described himself in an interview as small, but meaner than hell. He said that because he wasn't very big, he had to be a little bit tougher. What he lacked in size, he made up in aggressiveness and attitude.

He may have been mean as hell on the gridiron, but he certainly had a sweet side and a life outside football and the classroom. While at Emporia State on a blind date, he met the love of his life, Joan Bader. They were married the year after his graduation on August 22, 1954 at the First Christian Church in her hometown of Leroy, Kansas and celebrated their sixty-first wedding anniversary the August before my dad passed away. They were both teachers, and Dad began his coaching career right away at Baxter Springs High School.

My parents always seemed happy—their relationship solid. I envision them as newlyweds, just starting out on a shoestring budget, doing lesson plans at night and grading papers, my mom going to all his Friday night football games. Later, after having children, my mom stayed home to raise us but remained an active part of my dad's teaching and coaching world, planning and organizing events and gatherings for the coaches and players and of course, still going to all the Friday night games.

I was adopted in 1971 at three days old. Ten years after the birth of my older brother, Jeff, my father came up with the idea to adopt. I was born early, so when my parents' lawyer called to tell them I had arrived, they were completely unprepared. Mom was so anxious to see me, however, that she wanted to immediately drive the sixty miles from their home in Osawatomie to the University of Kansas Medical Center in Kansas City. Dad protested. I was jaundiced, which was considered more serious then than it is now, so he didn't want to get her hopes up in case something were to go wrong. That was him—always thinking about other people and trying to protect those he loved. Although I didn't find out about my adoption until I was twelve, I never felt different or separate from my family. My parents are my parents—blood or not.

Football occupied much of my dad's time, so my mom was in charge on the home front. We spent a great deal of time together in my dad's absence. I ran track in the summers, so she drove me all over the state for meets from the time I was in third grade on. She and I would drive to Leroy on weekends to be with Dad. I loved being with my mom, but I missed my dad, so time with him was extra special.

As I got older, Mom, Dad, and I took trips every Spring Break—amazing trips—Florida, California, Washington, Colorado, and Hawaii. By the time I was in high school, my dad was, in some ways, a bit of a local "celebrity," so it was always refreshing to get away and just be together as a family without the distractions of home. Once my

Jennifer and Bill Freeman in front of thier home in Lawrence, Kansas, circa 1978

brother and I were grown and gone, my parents continued to travel, but as much as they enjoyed that, I truly think my dad loved his farm in Leroy more than any other place in the world.

I grew up mostly in Lawrence, Kansas during Dad's sixteen-year coaching stint at Lawrence High School, but almost every single weekend, he would drive his old Ford truck down to Leroy where he and Mom had inherited land from my mom's parents. He would work the land, hunt for arrowheads, look for turkeys, and fish. It was his happy place, and the only place he wanted to be after a disappointing Friday night loss. If they won, he'd come home energized, talkative, anxious to look at film, but if they lost, he was quiet, reserved, and often drove out to Leroy in the middle of the night to clear his mind.

As a father, I looked up to him and saw him as my hero. When I was small, he seemed intimidating and scary, but as I grew up, I saw him as the big-hearted teddy bear he really was. He was soft-spoken but to the point, never mincing words. You always knew exactly where you stood with Bill Freeman.

I attended the same high school where my dad taught and coached, and I *loved* having him there as much as I *hated* having him there. I had a blast going to football practices, riding the bus to games with the team, and just hanging out in his office at random times throughout the school day. On the flipside, he knew *everything* that went on in that school, from my grades, to my schedule, to who I had a crush on. You name it, there were no secrets and no way a football player would ever date me because they were all terrified of him. One time, while he was reviewing film with the entire team, he let it slip that I had a crush on one of the players. I was mortified! He wouldn't even let me sit where I wanted to on the bus when I traveled with the team—I always had to sit up front next to one of the assistant coaches.

I couldn't get away with anything. During one of my business classes, I took advantage of the fact that we had a substitute and switched seats to be closer to one of my friends. As a result, I was marked absent that hour since I was not in my assigned seat, and if it didn't take more than fifteen minutes before my dad tracked me down in the hallway and took my car keys away. I tried to explain that I was actually present in class, but my pleas fell on deaf ears. There was no messing around with Dad.

In another instance, my friend and I wanted to be the official "water girls" for the team. We figured what better way to hang around a bunch of good looking football players. Well, that lasted all of ten minutes. We got into a big water fight, and Dad said, "That's it. You're done." Even when I got to be his teaching assistant my senior year, which I thought would be "so fun," he wrote me a pass every day to go to the library to study. I'm serious when I say I could not get away with anything!

Despite his reputation as a tough cookie, Dad had a smile that could light up a room. I saw it often after an exhilarating win, but when I told him that I was pregnant with my first child, the beaming smile that crept across his face will be forever emblazoned in my memory. It was an expression I had never quite seen before—disbelief, pride, amazement, joy.

For as good of a father as he was, he was an even better grandfather, involved from day one and always checking to make sure I was doing all the "right things" for my children—regular bed and bath times, healthy food, and reading among his top concerns. Dad often showed up unannounced to take the kids on nature walks or to the library for story time. As they got older, he took them to gather firewood or to fish. He tried to take me fishing when I was little, but he grew frustrated because he said I talked too much. He hoped to have better luck with my children.

As a man, Bill Freeman was the most unassuming character you can possibly imagine. Despite his success and local notoriety, he did not have one conceited bone in his body. Dad had money, but no one would've ever guessed it by his old, beat-up truck and our garage sale clothes. Even though he gave money generously to people who needed it, he was never a show-off or a bragger, and while he served as mayor of his beloved little Leroy for twenty-one years, he did so without a salary. He despised the limelight and was truly a simple, no frills kind of guy who practiced what he preached. He was always early, and he always went above and beyond in terms of effort and time. That genuineness is what people liked most about him.

Bill's tribute to his daughter Jennifer, which he painted on the side of the shed at the family home in Leroy, Kansas

Dad did not express his emotions very often and rarely said, "I love you," but he showed it in countless ways. One of my fondest memories was when he took me out to a shed on his farm in Leroy. He instructed me to walk into the shed and take a look at the east wall. While I found his directions slightly odd, I followed along and when I looked up at the wall, I saw my name, "Jenny" spray-painted in bright orange letters. Puzzled, I asked, "Why did you do this?"

"I was just thinking about you today," he replied matter of factly. That was his way of telling me he loved me. My bright orange monogram is still on that shed wall, and it brings a smile to my face today just as it did then. This seemingly small gesture was indicative of Dad's down to earth approach to everything, and I knew it meant far more than an expensive gift ever could. In his own humble way, Dad expressed great love for his family, his community, and his players in countless ways each and every day. It is the most important part of the legacy he leaves behind, far more impactful than his record setting winning seasons—love demonstrated not in flashy, self-absorbed displays, but in earnest and sincere acts of kindness and self-sacrifice. That's what made him a real winner, that's the heart of a true champion.

Chapter 2

Winning Record

*"Show class, have pride, and display character.
If you do, winning takes care of itself."*
Paul "Bear" Bryant

Dad's thirty-six-year coaching career began in 1954 at Baxter Springs, one of the smallest high schools in Kansas, and ended at Lawrence High School, the biggest in the Sunflower State at that time. The bulk of his career was spent at Osawatomie High School and Lawrence High School. Despite great success during his nine years at Osawatomie, including a perfect season and two state titles, when he was offered the position at Lawrence in 1974, it was a job he felt he couldn't refuse.

Lawrence was the powerhouse school in the state, and Dad was anxious for an opportunity to teach and coach at that level. He spent sixteen years in Lawrence, retiring from teaching

BILL FREEMAN
B. S. & M. S. in Education

Image of a young coach, Osawatomie, Kansas High School yearbook

and coaching in 1990 with a football record of 242-81-3, highlighted by eight state championship titles: one at Leroy High School, two at Osawatomie High School, and five at Lawrence. Five of his former players went on to play in the NFL, while over a hundred played in college and dozens of his former players and assistant coaches became head coaches and athletic directors.

In addition, he coached two track teams to state titles in his two final years at Lawrence High. In his entire career, he only had four losing seasons.

For all those thirty-six years, from August through November, Dad and his coaching staffs worked tirelessly, scouring reel after reel of film, scouting opponents, and devising plays. Dad scribbled notes about potential plays any and everywhere he could, on tiny bits and scraps of used paper and napkins that ended up strewn all over his office. His passion for football was like a voracious appetite that could never quite be satisfied. It kept him driving ahead, always striving for more and more success.

Coaching Fundamentals

Dad pushed his players in a similar fashion, always believing that they could do better. Scott Stidham described his experience and that of most of Dad's players when he said, "All weekend you'd hear how great you were because you'd just won, but he [Coach Freeman] was so thorough watching film, he could always find something you did wrong, and he'd show you."

Dad didn't do that out of spite or to embarrass his players. He pointed out their weaknesses in a genuine attempt to help them improve. He said it himself, "I wanted my players to get better. If they thought they were average, I wanted them to be good. If they thought they were good, I wanted them to be great." Repeatedly, he drilled into his players, "Never settle!"

Defense was key to winning a game. Dad always put his best athletes on defense, a strategy that obviously proved successful. Even when he had superstar quarterbacks, his focus was defense. His rational was straightforward: the other team can't win if they can't score.

Adaptation was another axiom Dad lived and coached by. "You've got to be like the sparrows and starlings," he told his athletes. "You don't want to be like the whooping crane. There are millions of sparrows and starlings. They adapted to the environment, but the whooping crane didn't adapt and now is almost extinct. You've got to adapt!"

He was extremely skilled at adapting to the team he had. Not all teams are created equal, so there were years when the talent was unmistakable, like his 1966 perfect season at Osawatomie with quarterback Lynn Dickey who played fifteen seasons in the NFL. Likewise, there were years when the talent was less impressive, but it didn't matter because Dad could motivate anyone, and he found ways to accentuate the positive attributes in every single player. He devised plays that maximized the team's strengths while minimizing their weaknesses.

Cam Miller, former quarterback at Lawrence High, remembers with deep appreciation the opportunity my dad gave him to play. "My senior year," Cam recalls, "we weren't expected to be very good." Cam was small, and there was a great deal of doubt surrounding him as quarterback, as well as the team in general that year. Fortunately for them, Dad did not approach coaching football in a one size fits all manner. He started from the ground up and built that 1986 team into state champions with his relentless work ethic—if you want to be better than the other guys, you work harder than the other guys. Dad believed in doing things a little bit longer, a little bit harder, with a little bit more intensity than everyone else. At Lawrence, they used a seven-man tackle sled instead of the typical five, they ran a mile after practice in full pads on the very first day, and no matter how rainy or frigid or sweltering the unpredictable Midwest weather might have been, they never skipped a day of practice.

No one on the team was exempt. Everyone on the team, from the quarterback to the kicker was expected to do every single drill with vigor, and it paid off in state titles. Cam credits Coach Freeman with believing in him when others doubted and teaching him to channel his own competitive drive and "fire" in the right direction. Like so many of my dad's former players, he sees now, in retrospect, that all the lessons he thought were just about football, were really about life.

"For a lot of us, he set the bar on what a work ethic looked like. The best lessons went far beyond the X's and O's of football," remembers former LHS lineman Kris Weidling, who played for the 1986 state title team that went 12-0. In an article by Gary Bedore in the *Lawrence Journal World* published shortly after Dad died, Kris said, "He did things like driving to get the game film at the earliest possible hour so he could watch it the maximum amount of times before discussing with the team. He also drew great parallels between the football field and life. In particular, I remember him stressing the importance of commitment by saying, 'It all starts here on the field with your teammates. If you quit here, you'll think it's okay to quit on your job or quit on your family.' When we won the state title, he said afterwards 'So now you know what it takes. There are those who have been here before and they've gone on to be dogs, and there have been those who have gone on to do great things. The choice is up to you.'"

Bill with Jeff Wright in front of Southern Cofffey County High School (formerly Leroy High School), circa 2007

Jeff Wright played at Lawrence from 1978-1982 and went on to play in the NFL as a nose tackle, appearing in all four of the Buffalo Bills' super bowls. He aptly describes Dad as "one of the best coaches to ever pick up a football." Admittedly a shy teenager who lacked guidance, Jeff says Dad took him under his wing, becoming a father figure to him and helping him grow up. Although Dad had a tough exterior, Jeff recalls that when he cracked his winning smile, you knew everything was okay. According to Jeff, Dad had a powerful impact on every one he came in contact with, touching lives forever through the game of football.

"G.E.E.T.U.S."

"Get some geetus!" Dad's high-pitched, squeaky voice would reverberate during practice if a player was slacking off or not following directions. It's not a real word, but like most of my father's "Freemanisms" (as they have become known), it bore real meaning, and every athlete who ever played football or ran track for my dad knows well what it stands for.

The "G" is for grit. Dad was tough, and he expected his players to be tough, too. He pushed them to play through the pain, often telling them, "I don't care about how big the other guy is across from you…go woop 'em!"

Lynn Dickey thought my dad was crazy during his first few practices at Osawatomie High School in 1965. Football programs didn't require the level of physical conditioning common today, so when Dad showed up and expected his team to run, they didn't know what to make of him. Lynn remembers sitting in the locker room after that first practice with his fellow teammates, looking at each other in disbelief and wondering, "Who is this guy?"

Of course, like all my dad's teams would eventually do, they soon learned the value of being physically fit and came to appreciate my dad's approach of "out toughing" the opponent. For Dad, that went beyond physical strength. He understood that most games are won or lost mentally, so he invested time in preparing his players mentally to beat their opponents. That was the real source of grit—mental prowess. If you had that, you would likely win both in football and in life.

Many of Dad's former players credit this mental toughness to their successes off the football field. Scott Stidham, who played for my dad at Lawrence in the late eighties, defines that mental toughness as the ability to walk away from difficult situations and the capacity to stand by your commitments. Other players have commented over the years that Dad introduced the notion of mental toughness to them and taught them to be mentally tough in ways they had never imagined they could be.

Lynn, who would've described himself as a "grinder" before meeting my dad, credits Dad with pushing him further than he ever thought possible. As a young boy in an era when moms called their kids home for dinner at dusk, Lynn always hated it when the neighborhood football game had to break up so everyone could scurry home. "It drove me crazy," he said, "when the other boys would leave before the game was finished." If finishing the game meant getting in trouble for coming home late, Lynn would opt for completing the game any day, but he was usually alone in his "never quit" attitude; that is, until he met Bill Freeman.

"Bill pushed me further and taught me how to be mentally tougher than I ever thought I could be," Lynn recalls. Lynn indicated that even when he was injured at times throughout his fifteen-year NFL career, it never dawned on him to quit. "That," he says, "is because of Bill Freeman."

The "E" is for excellence. Dad didn't necessarily believe in perfection, but he certainly believed in practice. Fundamentals were the key to victory, and he believed in keeping things simple. His teams didn't run sophisticated, complicated plays. They had a handful of basic plays that they executed with proficiency, and if they did not, Bill Freeman would keep them practicing until they did.

Dad paid attention to details, and he wanted things done a certain way. The small things, the nuances of the game, mattered. During one Lawrence High practice, the players just weren't getting a play quite right. Dad wasn't going to let anyone leave until they did, but as the afternoon turned to evening, it grew dark on the unlit practice field. Determined to finish what he'd started, Dad had the players and all the coaches pull their cars up close and shine their lights on the practice field. Using a flashlight to read his notes, Dad continued drilling the play until they got it right.

The second "E" stands for everyone. Dad treated everyone equally and fairly. His former players always say that, and I know it to be true in Dad's life off the football field as well. Chris King, who played at Lawrence remembers, "Coach treated us all the same…whether you were an All-State player, fourth string, or a guy who never got in a game at all. Everyone was equally important to the success of the team."

In the same Gary Bedore article from December of 2015 mentioned earlier, Jan-Eric Anderson, a three-year letterman in track and field, recalled, "My memory of Coach is of a man who expected great things to come from great effort. We had so many talented athletes on that team, and he expected them to give everything they had. He was a motivator. Coach had a way of getting you to believe you could give more and achieve more. And he had that impact on guys who were state champions in their events, as well as the guys that struggled to stay with the pack at the jv meets. He connected with everyone he coached."

Ron Commons, who coached alongside Dad the entire time he was at Lawrence, remembers that Dad made a concerted effort to give everyone a chance to play, even if they weren't necessarily a star. Dad found places for his athletes to shine. If they couldn't be a hero on offense or defense, then maybe they could be a hero on special teams, and whenever possible, he brought younger players up and gave them the opportunity to learn.

He also called everyone out equally. "That's how you knew he cared," remembers Jeff Wright.

When Dad took the job in Lawrence in 1974, like so many other high schools in America, Lawrence High had endured its share of wounds from the racial division and political tension that punctuated the early seventies. He walked into not only an ailing football program, but an ailing culture, struggling to rebuild and integrate in the aftermath of conflict. In his typical style, Coach Freeman made no distinctions between races. The best players played, no matter what. The fairness and respect with which he treated his players quickly made great strides to reunite the Lawrence High student body and rebuild the football program.

One of Dad's volunteer trainers, Don Gardner, better known to many as "Red Dog," praises Dad for never picking on players or bullying them, as some coaches did back in the day. Don also recalls how supportive my dad was of girls' athletics at a time when Title IX was still relatively new. As those close to him know, my dad's true love of sport was track and field. While he may not be as well-known for his victories there, it was his passion, and he regard-

Bill Freeman, Lawrence High School football game, sometime in the 1980s

ed his runners with the same level of admiration and respect as he did his football players. Everyone mattered to my dad.

The "T" stands for tenacity. Dad did not give up easily nor accept defeat without a fight. He inspired his players to leave it all out on the field. Bob Whitehead, who played for Dad in 1961 at Leroy High School and then went on to coach alongside Dad at Osawatomie, remembers one particular game against another small-town rival when he ran into a player so hard he got the wind knocked out of him. He said Dad's only question to him was, "Bob, can you play?" Bob couldn't even speak, but he wasn't about to admit to my dad that he couldn't finish the game.

Dad was tenacious when it came to winning, but he was also tenacious in the way he kept his word. If he said it, he meant it. In 1981, a running back from a rival high school bragged that he would rush for fifteen hundred yards that season. Lawrence High School was scheduled to play his team in the final game of the season, and by the time it rolled around, the running back was only fifty-one short yards away from reaching his goal. Dad, along with the entire Lawrence High team and coaching staff, wanted nothing more than to thwart this overconfident player's efforts. Dad promised the team that if they could keep the running back from hitting the fifteen hundred yard benchmark, he would shave his head.

Lawrence's defense rose to the challenge, holding the runner to only forty-six yards that game, five precious yards away from his goal. "Men," Dad declared at practice the following Monday, "I am a man of my word." To the team's surprise, he lifted his stocking cap to reveal a very shiny, freshly bald head.

Jeff Wright gives Dad the credit for teaching him to never give up. After being recruited to play at Tulsa University, Jeff returned home after his second year dissatisfied having to play offensive guard. He opted for work over school for eight months until he realized what he had given up, the mistake he had made in leaving school and throwing away an opportunity to play ball. He remembered Coach Freeman's lessons: you only get something out of it if you put something in and not everything in life is going to work out the way you want it to. It's how you react to life's disappointments that matters.

Jeff took those words to heart and got busy. He got back in shape, played at Coffeyville Junior College, received a full ride scholarship at Central Missouri State University where they retired his jersey, and went on to play seven seasons in the NFL. Bill Freeman was a man who never gave up, and he inspired that kind of tenacity in all his players.

"U" is for understanding. First and foremost, my dad had an innate understanding of people, which is what made him such an excellent coach. He understood his players, his fellow coaches, and his opponents. He knew what it took to win, and he understood his and others' limitations with such depth and clarity that he was able to win despite obvious obstacles.

While coaching Lynn Dickey at Osawatomie High School, Dad understood the importance of keeping Dickey and his scholarship arm safe from sacks, so he devised strategies to ensure that the team protected their star quarterback. If a receiver dropped a pass, the penalty was a lap around the track. If an offensive lineman gave up a sack during a game, the stakes were even higher. He would be required to take a snap at the next practice while all the backs and receivers got to tackle him. This approach worked—Dickey was spared senseless hits and the team went on that year to be undefeated state champs.

Dad was also an excellent judge of character. He could read people in the first instant he met them and almost always ended up being right. He truly believed the best about everyone and wanted the best for everyone. Being of small stature, he had a soft spot for smaller players and believed that they could be just

as strong as the bigger guys. He always said, "It ain't the size of the dog in the fight, it's the size of the fight in the dog." It was all about heart, and if you had heart, Coach Freeman could see it and he would give you the chance to play. "The players I remember may not have had the best abil-

Lawrence High School student Charlie Bowen with Bill during a game, 1988

ity," Dad told Kurt Caywood, a Lawrence reporter, in 1990, "but they were the ones who had the biggest heart."

Clearly, Dad's players saw his heart and valued that more than the many titles he amassed. When he was still teaching and coaching, his office was often occupied by former players dropping in for a visit or current students just hanging out. Dad understood teenagers, was passionate about teaching and coaching, and loved all his students and athletes.

Finally, "S" is for smiles. Dad had a smile that could melt even the Grinch's heart. He was selective about when he flashed it, but when he did, it felt like sunshine flooded the room. Despite the fact that he was serious about most things most of the time, he could be funny, and he often was without even trying to be.

One of Dad's former players and fellow coaches, Bob Lisher, shares the story of one such time when Dad was not necessarily trying to be funny. He was in the middle of one of his emotional, amped-up, pre-game motivational speeches when all the sudden, his gum flew out of his mouth and landed on the floor in front of him. No one knew if it was okay to laugh or not, so they all sat there in silence. After a momentary pause, Dad smiled, leaned down to pick up his gum, placed it back in his mouth, and carried on with his speech.

Another former Lawrence High player, Keith Cobb, remembers, "Every Sunday afternoon during the season, we would watch films from the previous Friday night's game in one of the classrooms at the school. During these years, we had the old reel film projector that was big and bulky. Coach would set the projector in the middle of the room and sit on top of a desk to run the film. One Sunday, he was having some problems with the film tape, and as he was trying to fix it, the whole projector fell off the desk and Coach went with it and fell to the ground with the projector. We all tried our hardest not to laugh out loud."

That's how it was with Dad—you didn't always know if he was being funny on purpose or not, so sometimes you weren't sure if you should laugh. The truth is, he had a great sense of humor and did not take himself too seriously, as evidenced by his numerous other funny sayings.

Other Freemanisms

There are too many to mention here, but the following are some favorites. If a player wasn't moving fast enough, he might hear, "You run like a dry creek!" If he wasn't playing smart, he might be on the receiving end of something like this, "If your brain were dynamite, you wouldn't make a pop," or perhaps, "You're like a turd in a punchbowl—you're out of place!"

If there was one thing that Dad had no patience for, it was players not giving one hundred percent. If someone was slacking off, not "hungry" enough, Dad would holler, "You put me in a barrel and you in a barrel and a sandwich in a barrel, and you would starve!" If he wanted to see more fight, he might shout, "You're either a lover or a fighter—which is it?" or "You couldn't fight your way out of a wet paper bag!"

He knew how to handle players who got a little too big in the britches as well. To thwart someone's conceited attitude, he would say, "That's not muscle, looks like water weight to me," or "You look like Tarzan, but you play like Jane!" And when players were getting noticed by recruiters and receiving press attention, he made sure to keep them in line with, "Stop wearin' your headlines on your helmet."

Dad also knew how to handle players and parents who were difficult. He understood that sometimes, you just weren't going to win an argument or convince someone else of your position. He often remarked, "You can't tell a fool he's a fool," and "You can't get into a pissing match with a skunk." As I said, he was an astute judge of character, so it wasn't often that you could fool him. He saw into people's hearts and knew exactly who he was dealing with. "You can polish a turd and polish a turd," he would shake his head, "but when you're done polishing, you still have a turd."

During games, Dad's "Freemanisms" would creep into his play calling and strategizing. "Open the gate!" was what running backs would hear when they were about to be tackled on the sidelines. It meant they were supposed to go attack and not run out of bounds. If a player seemed to be looking too far downfield or too far ahead in the game, Dad would yell, "Don't run by Peter to block Paul!" And anytime the team's success was on the line, you could hear Dad's piercing pitch, "Don't dink it up!"

Sometimes, when Dad was angry or frustrated, his "Freemanisms" wouldn't come out quite right, which made them that much more humorous. Chris King remembers what happened during halftime of the 1987 quarterfinal game against Olathe North. The players were well prepared for that game and should have been winning at the half, but they had suffered a couple turnovers, so the mood was heavy as they filed into the locker room. Chris and the other players were expecting the usual halftime talk from Dad—a little motivation mixed in with a little chewing out— but instead, Dad was speechless. In the silence, he paced back and forth a few times, shook his head, threw down his roll of plays, and spewed, "You guys are playing like a bunch of dog-sucking eggs!"

What he meant to say, of course, was "egg-sucking dogs." According to Chris, you could've heard a pin drop in that locker room. "Oh hell," Dad picked back up after a long pause, "You know what I mean!" Apparently, they did because they rallied and went on to win that game, qualifying for the state play-offs.

After games, Dad's "Freemanisms" would also creep into conversation. Everyone remembers with a smile what he would say to the team on long bus rides when they stopped at Burger King on the way home. "All right," he would direct, "go on inside and get yourselves a wooper and a middle drink." Everytime I think of it, I still chuckle—who says "wooper" for "Whopper" and "middle drink" for "medium?" Bill Freeman, that's who.

Embedded in his often politically incorrect remarks were also nuggets of wisdom and life advice: "Cream rises to the top. You get out of it what you put in. If you didn't screw up, you wouldn't have to apologize. You're the captain of your own ship. You control your own destiny." These adages echo in my mind today as clearly as they did thirty years ago, and I know the same is true for many others. Dad's quirky words truly shaped peoples' lives.

Stroke of Mischief

There is no doubt that Dad had a mischievous side. Not everybody had the opportunity to see it, but those who did will never forget it.

Scott Stidham shares this memorable moment from the 1989 track season, "When I was a senior during track and field, I pulled a muscle in my hip flexor. Since I couldn't practice, I was writing times down for Coach at our time trial practice. He had the starter pistol in his hand and had just sent the last group on their two-hundred-meter time trial. He told me to look, and over by the fence, there was a rabbit eating some grass. He walked over quietly and got down gently right near it, held the gun toward it, and shot the blank. That rabbit took off faster than I've ever seen a rabbit run! Coach looked at me with this big smile on his face and said, 'I bet that rabbit thought I was a pretty poor shot.'"

Lynn Dickey also recounts a hilarious episode with my dad that took him by surprise. Prior to this experience, he had only known my dad to be the hard-nosed, no-nonsense coach he saw every day in practice. That all changed when Dad invited Lynn to watch the University of Kansas play Kansas State University in Manhattan, Kansas in the fall of 1966. Lynn had always dreamed of attending KU, so he jumped at the chance to fly with my dad from Osawatomie to Manhattan in a little three-seater plane owned by a gentleman in town. During the short flight, Lynn inquired about the location of their seats in the stadium only to find out that Dad didn't have tickets. Lynn was a little concerned and asked on the cab ride from the airport to the stadium, "Mr. Freeman, what are we gonna do?"

I don't know what my dad's answer was, but Lynn said that once they arrived, my dad proceeded to scale a ten-foot barbed wire fence to get into the stadium. "Be careful," he shouted down to Lynn. "Don't put your hand on the barb when you climb over."

Lynn remembers being dumbfounded. He couldn't believe that Mr. Freeman had just scaled a fence as if it were no big deal to sneak into a college football game. "It was a big deal for a rule-following high school kid," Lynn jokes. "This was way out of my comfort zone!"

The story continues. Once over the fence, they still had to get through the gates, and they still had no tickets. No problem for Bill Freeman. They averted the gates and headed to the west side of the stadium, directly to the towering ladder that led to the top of the press box where the camera crews sat in the "crow's nest." He urged young Lynn to climb up with him, and from this bird's eye view, Dad spotted some empty seats way down below, so they made their way down and scooted in on the bleachers much closer to the action. Without tickets, Lynn got to watch his favorite college football team and returned home with a great Mr. Freeman story to tell all his friends. It shocked him at the time because he had never seen that side of Dad, but now Lynn says he thinks Dad got a kick out of doing "ornery things." I think he's right.

Learning How to Lose

Dad certainly won more than he lost, but in football, like life, you can't win 'em all. He believed it was just as important to teach his players how to lose as it was to win. In 1985, everyone expected Lawrence High to be the 6A Kansas State Champions. They had done it the year before and had an even more talented squad assembled, ready to claim victory in '85, but it didn't happen. In a stunning loss to Shawnee Mission West in the final playoff game at Lawrence High, they kissed the chance at a state title good-bye. Trainer Don Gardner recalls the crushing disappointment as all the boys assembled in the gym after the game in their muddy gear, awaiting the final post-game analysis from Coach Freeman.

Dad believed in callin' it like you see it and was not a man to mince words. "You stunk it up," he stated matter of factly. "You didn't play good football. You didn't deserve to win. You didn't do what you came here to do today." Dad went on, "But you know what? I didn't do a good job today either. I didn't coach you as well as I should have." He continued to name all the various men on his coaching staff and pointed out how they had all failed. He even called out Don, "And you know what? I don't think ol' Red Dog taped you up as good as he could've either."

Don was slightly offended but got the point. Dad took just as much ownership for the devastating loss as anyone else on the team and expected everyone on the team to do the same. He didn't blame one or two players for mistakes or one or two coaches for failed strategies or any of the referees for incorrect calls. No single player or coach or call wins a game, and no single player or coach or call loses a game. They were a team—win and lose.

Like a family, you take the bad with the good and you keep moving forward. For Dad, once the game was over, it was over. You moved on, and in this case, that meant moving on to prepare for the next year, when Lawrence did, in fact, win the state championship game against rival Junction City. The smile on Dad's face when they won in 1986 is something I'll never forget.

Career Highlights

Bill Freeman is still considered one of the winningest coaches in Kansas high school football history, with an impressive two hundred, forty-two career wins. His eight state football championships include two before the playoff system was introduced, one at Leroy in 1962 and one at Osawatomie in 1966. Following the institution of state-wide playoffs in 1969, Dad won one more at Osawatomie in 1973 and the remaining five at Lawrence in 1979, 1984, 1986, 1987, and 1989.

In addition to two perfect seasons at Osawatomie in 1966 and 1973 and one in Lawrence in 1986, many of Dad's Lawrence teams completed close to perfect seasons. The 1984 team, which included Keith DeLong, an NFL first round draft pick, went 11-1, allowing only two field goals in the final eight games of the season and defeating Manhattan 29-3 in the state match up. Finishing 10-1, the 1985 team claimed the school's five hundredth win. In 1987, the Lawrence Chesty Lions won the school's twenty-first state championship, defeating their undefeated rival, the Manhattan Indians, 17-12, and in 1988, although they lost to Manhattan in the championship game, they ended the season 10-2. In Dad's final season at Lawrence in 1989, they ended 11-1 and once again defeated their nemesis, Manhattan, reclaiming the 6A State title.

Ron Commons coached with Dad at Lawrence and later went on to become the athletic director. In his opinion, Dad's most significant win was the first State title he had at Lawrence in 1979. That year, the championship game was played at Haskell Field in Lawrence. It was a rare occasion and one that hasn't happened since. It was a big deal to have the home field advantage and the home crowd support against one of Lawrence's biggest rivals, Wichita Southeast, a team that had won the title the last two years in a row. It was a nail-biting match up that ended in a crazy Lawrence play. The quarterback and the end who received he ball were the only ones on the field who moved.

It resulted in a touchdown and a Lawrence victory. It was the beginning of a long run of state championships for Lawrence under my dad's direction.

In the opinion of many others, the undefeated season of 1986 was the highlight of Dad's career. Led by Kansas player-of-the-year, quarterback Lance Flachsbarth, the Chesty Lions finished 12-0, beating Junction City 20-7 for the state championship. National Scholastic Sports ranked Lawrence the eighteenth best high school team in the country.

That very well may have been the highlight of Dad's career, but if you would've asked him, he would've likely told you that his proudest accomplishment from his nearly four-decade career was winning two consecutive Kansas State titles in track and field at Lawrence High. The first of those two in 1989 was the school's first ever title in boys' track. He loved coaching track, so it was a truly fitting end to his career to take the boys' track team all the way to two state victories.

Dad loved coaching, period, and he loved his athletes. His greatest joy was when athletes came back after graduation to share their stories of success beyond the athletic arena. In an interview with Gary Bedore of the *Lawrence Journal World* in 2012, Dad said, "When they'd come up to me later in life to tell me they were glad I was tough on them, it made me proud. I knew then I'd helped make a difference."

I don't think there's any doubt in anyone's mind that Bill Freeman made a difference and that his "winning record" on the field was reflected in his winning record off it.

Chapter 3
No Rest in Retirement

"The price of success is hard work, dedication to the job at hand, and the determination that whether we win or lose, we have applied the best of ourselves to the task at hand"
Vince Lombardi

No one expected Dad to retire when he did, least of all me, but there were probably clues along the way that we all missed. Ron Oelschlager, quarterback of the 1989 team that won Dad his last state title, remembers emotions running high the week before that final game. Dad called him down to his office, fuming mad. Ron was terrified, wondering what he had done to anger my father. As it turned out, Dad just wanted to watch film with Ron. He had just gotten off the phone with the coach of the opposing team whom he did not like very much, and he was fit to be tied. Dad told Ron, "I called you down here to watch film so we could kick their ass!"

In retrospect, I am sure my dad knew this was going to be the last time he coached a football team, and he wanted his final game to be a state championship win. At the end of the last practice before the state match-up, Dad called the team in and began his usual pre-game talk that always included a reminder to the boys that "it's just a game." Ron recalls that as Dad was saying the words, "It's just a game," he stopped himself, paused, and with tears streaming down his face, proclaimed, "Oh to hell with that! I want you to kick their ass this weekend!" It was the perfect rallying cry, and that is exactly what they did, winning my dad his last Kansas State football championship.

Just a few short months later in February of 1990, he was quoted in a *Lawrence Journal World* article, "After thirty-six years, I think I coached and taught long enough." Announcing that he would retire at the end of that school year, Dad admitted, "I contemplated resigning several years ago, but I kind of made up my mind this year during the last part of the season. It's a hard decision, but I've got to quit sometime. I'd rather quit when I still feel good about the game and teaching, and I still do."

So, after one more state track championship in May of 1990, my dad's long and storied coaching career came to an end, and at age fifty-nine, he began the next chapter. It was a chapter in his life marked by the same spirit of hard work and determination as the previous one and one that never took him too far away from the town, the people, and the sports he loved.

Upon announcing his retirement, which was as much a surprise to me as it was to everyone else, Dad and Mom began making plans to move back to Leroy permanently. Dad was anxious to get busy and be more hands on at the bank he had owned since 1979 and on the land that he and my mom had owned since her parents' deaths. He tried to encourage me to move with them, but I was a young adult, out on my own for the first time, and I had zero interest in the tiny town of Leroy, Kansas, population six hundred. I decided to stayed in Lawrence, heart-broken that my dad's coaching career was over. It was literally all I had ever known, and I wasn't ready for it to come to an end.

He was though, and people were happy for him. I guess he knew it was time, and he jumped right in once they got settled. He loved his land—all three thousand acres of it. They grew corn, beans, and wheat in addition to enrolling a good portion of the land in the Farm Service Agency's Conservation Reserve Program (CRP). The aim of this program is to reestablish vital land cover to help improve water quality, prevent soil erosion, and reduce the loss of wildlife habitats. Essentially, this meant leaving those portions of land unfarmed to restore the natural prairie grasses. Dad was a true conservationist at heart, so he whole-heartedly supported anything he could do to protect the natural habitat and preserve the land. To this day, many acres of his property are still devoted to the CRP.

It was not uncommon during his so called "retirement" to find him riding his Allis-Chalmers tractor, tilling the land himself or taking long walks to spot turkeys, quail, or deer. Dad was not a hunter. He liked to see animals in the wild, watch and observe them. He possessed a certain sense of awe and wonder at nature, a reverence and maybe even a connection that seemed to run deeper in him than in most people.

He also had a passion for history, specifically that of his native Kansas, which was originally inhabited by the Osage,

Kansa, Kiowa, Arapaho, Pawnee, and Comanche Indian tribes. Dad had an abiding appreciation for the Native American roots of the land and one of his all-time favorite activities was arrowhead hunting. He could find an arrowhead almost anywhere, and over the course of his lifetime,

Bill with arrowhead display at the First National Bank of Leroy, Kansas, sometime in the mid 1990s

amassed quire an impressive collection.

He always tried to get me to go with him when I was a kid, but I often declined. Arrowhead hunting just wasn't my thing. I did find one once though, or at least Dad let me think I did. I was so excited and believed it was a real arrowhead for many years. I was well into adulthood when he finally broke it to me that it was only a rock. I guess he hadn't wanted to squelch my enthusiasm in hopes that I might be motivated to go hunting with him again. I know now that he was just trying to find ways to spend time with me.

One Leroy native who did enjoy arrowhead hunting with Dad was Jeff True. Jeff remembers that at first, Dad was secretive about where he found his arrowheads. He was quick to show them off to Jeff, but slow to reveal his prime locations. As they became better friends and Dad's trust grew, he began to share every single detail of each find with Jeff.

Jeff's fondest memory is one afternoon when Dad invited him over to see his entire collection. They sat on the living room floor for hours while Dad unloaded cigar box after cigar box full of precious and priceless arrowheads. "A privilege" is how Jeff describes that day and that experience. Dad's collection was close to his heart, and I don't think he shared it with many people, so Jeff is probably right—that was, indeed, a privilege.

It might sound as if Dad was leisurely enjoying his retirement, spending time on his land and hunting arrowheads, but that is not an accurate depiction of what this time in his life looked like. "Retirement" for dad involved a full-time job as president of the First National Bank of Leroy. He purchased the bank in 1979, but while coaching in Lawrence, he employed someone else to run the day-to-day business. Once he moved back to Leroy, he took the reins full time, trading in his tennis shoes and coaching whistle for dress pants and dress shoes. True to form, Dad arrived early every day before his other employees and took an active role in every facet of the business. No job was too small. If it got busy, he would work the window or answer the phone, whatever needed to be done.

I am very familiar with "Bill Freeman, the banker" because from 1991-2011, I worked for Dad at the bank. I know I said I wasn't interested in moving to the tiny town of Leroy, but that was before I fell in love with a man from Leroy, and that changed everything. Suddenly, the little dot on the map without a stoplight seemed more appealing. I wouldn't trade that decision for anything. It meant I got to spend every day for twenty years working alongside my dad. It wasn't always easy, but it was precious time to me now that he's gone.

When your dad is the bank president, there are obvious perks to the job, but the best was that he would let me bring my children to work. He was a doting grandfather and loved spending time with my three kids. He would let them "help" and sometimes even took them with him to Kansas City to the Federal Reserve. He also allowed me the flexibility I needed when the kids were sick or had appointments.

Dad was an excellent boss. He was kind-hearted and generous, but tough. I was always late, and I know it drove him crazy. He would shake his head and say, "Jenny, I'm gonna have to let you go." Of course, I knew he wasn't serious, but his expectations of me helped me to grow up. There were many life lessons during this time. He would catch my attention and say, "Come in my office." I always knew some sort of "talk" was about to ensue in which he was going to offer me advice about marriage or child-rearing. He often scolded me, telling me I needed an "attitude adjustment." He was usually right—I did.

He encouraged me often, reminding me that I am the captain of my own ship, that I control my own destiny. He reminded me whenever I was feeling sorry for myself that there are people out there who have it much worse. "You get out of it what you put in," he always said and often chided me to "Get some smarts" and "Stop dinkin' around." Most importantly, he called on me to put others before myself, which I witnessed him do day after day, both in his personal and professional life.

Dad's love for the town and people of Leroy led him to run for mayor in 1993, a post he occupied for the next twenty-one years. Refusing a salary that entire time, he met monthly with the five-member City Council to help ensure Leroy's lasting success. Although unassuming, Leroy is home to multiple million-dollar businesses with national and international operations as well as one of the largest greenhouses in the state of Kansas.

Thanks to Dad's love of history and his desire to create some sort of tourist attraction in the town of Leroy, it also now boasts a dual memorial in City Park to former populist Kansas governor, John Leedy, and Lower Creek Indian leader, Yahola. The memorial, which holds bronze plaques recalling the fact that both men had been residents of Leroy, was built next to the Veterans' Memorial in City Park in 2000. It was a project near and dear to the heart of Mayor Freeman.

He was involved in the community in other ways as well, serving as a Deacon at the First Christian Church of Leroy. He was active in the Coffey County Historical Society and the Allen County Community College Endowment Association and was a member of Neosho Lodge, number twenty-seven. Besides his passion for arrowheads, he also collected coins, bank notes, and currency and was often invited to share that, along with his love of history, with various classes at the high school. He also loved to work with other area coaches to train and inspire leadership in their athletes.

In his spare time, when he wasn't farming his three thousand acres, banking, or running the town, Dad and Mom traveled. He loved to see the world. In addition to traveling stateside, they also went on exotic excursions to the United Kingdom and China, but his favorite destination was Hot Springs, Arkansas. Dad suffered from debilitating migraine headaches his entire life, and the hot spring baths in Arkansas were one of the few things that provided him any relief.

You knew not to bother Dad when he was having a migraine for fear he'd bite your head off. When Bob Lisher was coaching with Dad at Lawrence, he came upon him one day in the locker room hanging from a pipe in the ceiling with two towels, one around the front under his chin and the other behind his head. Bob panicked, thinking that Dad had hung himself. It turned out he had rigged a way to give himself homemade traction to alleviate his headache. Sounds like something Dad would do, but I'm glad in his later years he opted for hot springs instead.

Football ran in Dad's blood, so even though he was no longer coaching, he frequently drove up to Lawrence to watch the Friday night showdown and often ended up in the stands siting with former players and reminiscing. Sometimes he went to watch his former players compete in college; many of them remembering him periodically on the sidelines at K-State, KU, and the other nearby colleges and universities.

While attending the University of Chicago, one of Dad's former track athletes, Ken Wang, even received a special surprise visit from my dad and mom. They were traveling through Chicago and decided to drop in on Ken studying in the library one afternoon. Ken shared the story with Gary Bedore, who reprinted it in the *Lawrence Journal World* on December 18, 2015, the day my father died.

Ken says when he heard Dad's distinctive voice calling his name, "Ken Wang! Ken Wang!" he thought he must be hallucinating from the long hours spent studying. He could hardly believe that my dad would go to all the trouble of tracking him down on campus just to say hello. My parents took him to dinner that evening, and Ken remembers being so struck by their genuine concern and care. All my parents wanted was to make sure he was doing okay in school. Dad wanted to know if he could do anything for him while they were in town.

Other players recall visiting Dad after he retired for dinner at his house and keeping in touch with him over the phone. If invited, Dad even attended weddings of former players. So many of them cherish his influence in their lives beyond high school football. He truly cared, and that didn't stop just because someone graduated or he retired. Even in Leroy, he kept his finger on the pulse of the football team there, often stopping players on the street to see how things were going and to inquire about how they were doing academically. He told them to keep their grades up and to always do the right thing. Once a coach, always a coach...even in retirement.

Chapter 4

The Unwinnable Game: Battling Alzheimer's

"Success is never final, failure is never fatal.
It's courage that counts. "
John Wooden

I knew what Alzheimer's was, but I would've never imagined in a million years that Dad would succumb to this debilitating disease. It happened slowly, so slowly in fact, that for quite a long time, I was in total denial that anything was wrong.

Dad was a giant in my eyes, indestructible. He had already proven himself to be indomitable, surviving a four-wheeler accident, a quadruple by-pass in 1995, and again in 2000, when he was diagnosed with prostate cancer. I will admit, the bypass surgery was frightening and one of the first times I had ever seen my father as less than invincible.

It all started one afternoon when he was scooping grain out of the back of a grain truck and complained that his arm was hurting. Not thinking much about it, he went out on his usual long walk, and before he got very far, turned around and headed back to the house, telling my mom that he felt like he couldn't walk. These were symptoms he knew not to ignore any further. Luckily, one of Dad's former players was a cardiologist in Kansas City and was able to get him in immediately the next day.

I planned to accompany my parents to the appointment, but Dad insisted I go to work instead. He assured me everything was going to be fine, but when I called Mom over my lunch break, I quickly learned that things were far from fine. Through muffled tears, she told me that they had admitted Dad to the hospital and that he would undergo a quadruple bypass the following morning.

Seeing him in recovery after the surgery was the first time I had ever seen my dad as anything less than the force of nature he was. Lying lifeless in that hospital bed with tubes attached everywhere and his eyes closed, he looked so small and helpless. I couldn't bear seeing him that way. That was not my father.

Being the man of few words that he was, he didn't verbalize what he was going

Bill and Joan Freeman at their 50th Wedding Anniversary celebration, Leroy, Kansas, 2004

through during that time, but I imagine he was taking stock and coming to terms with his own mortality. It was sobering for all of us, but I didn't know how to help him. The only thing I knew that *did* brighten his spirits was Tyler, my oldest and the only grandchild at the time. Once Dad was home, I took him to see Dad often and he always brought a smile to Dad's face.

After four or five months, Dad started coming in the bank more frequently, slowly working his way back to full days and his regular schedule. It was so nice to have him back that it didn't take long for me to forget all about these health scares. Dad was back to his normal self, going a hundred miles an hour, and all seemed right with the world.

On an intellectual level, you know that your parents aren't going to live forever, so in my mind, I knew that at some point, his age would catch up to him and he would probably get sick. I assumed maybe it would be another form of cancer or more heart problems that would eventually end his life. I never dreamt that it would be Alzheimer's.

When it began, it was subtle. At the bank, there would be deposits missing or things out of place. Dad started having trouble recalling people's names, so much so that he eventually told me he couldn't work the window anymore. It was embarrassing for him not to remember names of people he had known for years.

Alzheimer's is deceptive, though. Some days, Dad seemed perfectly fine, and he was in his seventies by this point. People forget things, right? Even those of us in middle age forget names and have trouble with word recall at times. It was difficult to discern in the beginning – is this normal aging, or is this something more? The answer to that is naturally blurred by our own perceptions and emotions. I didn't want to believe that this was anything more than the normal forgetfulness that comes with getting older.

Over time, it became clearer and more difficult to ignore. On many occasions, Dad left the house and didn't tell my mother where he was going. That may not have bothered her years before, but now, it was becoming a frightening proposition. What if he got lost? We wouldn't even know where to begin to look for him. Or worse, what if he got into an accident and hurt himself or someone else?

One afternoon, when leaving the market in Burlington, Dad mistakenly got into someone else's car and drove off. The vehicle's owner notified the police, assuming her car had been stolen. Luckily, the officer knew our family, so when he found Dad in the "stolen" car, he called Mom right away.

The writing was on the wall. It was time to take away his keys. It was the hardest thing I have ever had to do, and I cried the whole time. "I'm not doing this to hurt you," I sobbed. "I'm doing this to protect you."

He was furious, and it didn't take long for him to find the keys where Mom had hidden them and get right back out on the road. We knew we had to do something, but Bill Freeman was a stubborn man. The straw that broke the camel's back was one morning when he placed a bowl of oatmeal under the broiler in the oven and left it. Fortunately, my brother, Jeff, was home and found it before any damage was done, but it became a real matter of safety from that point forward.

There was no way we could've broached the subject with Dad that perhaps he had Alzheimer's, but we were able to convince him that it was time for a "check-up." I will never forget that appointment. I don't know if I actually expected it to go differently than it did, but I guess I didn't expect things to move so quickly. That day changed everything.

We sat nervously in Dr. Shell's office as he went through the motions of a regular check-up. Then, he proceeded to ask my dad a series of simple questions. In response to the question, "What year is it?" Dad replied, "1985." It was 2010. My heart sank.

He didn't know who the president was or the date of his own birthday. When Dr. Shell asked him to draw the hands of a clock face inside a circle on a piece of paper, he was unable to do so and looked at us with an expression of sheer helplessness and despair. The worst part was that there was absolutely nothing we do to help him. He was looking to us for answers, and there were none. There was absolutely nothing we could do for him.

We took Dad home feeling utterly defeated and lost. We knew enough about the disease to know that it would become progressively worse, and we knew that at some point, Dad would not be able to remain in the house with Mom. In that moment, though, it was all too much to take in. For as long as possible, we all tried to carry on as close to "normal" as we could.

The cat was out of the bag, so to speak, as it was now no secret that Dad was suffering from Alzheimer's. It was a relief to be able to talk about it and share it with others. Obviously, we hadn't been the only ones noticing Dad's cognitive decline, and with Leroy being the close-knit community it is, it was comforting to know that there were people all around keeping a watchful and loving eye on Dad as he continued to go about his daily routine.

In late 2010, he sold the bank, which meant more free time for him. In an article for the *Topeka Capital-Journal* in July of that year, Dad told reporter Kevin Haskins, "People ask me if I'd do it all over again, buy the bank." He continued, "I tell them, 'Yes, but I'd have to be a little younger.'" He added, "We've had good years."

In early 2012, Dad stepped down as mayor after twenty-one years. Several months later, he told reporter, Gary Bedore, "Millions of people are losing their memory, not just one but a lot of people." Dad was keenly aware of the scope of this disease and did not want anyone to feel sorry for him. In that same interview, he admitted to Bedore that Alzheimer's had slowed him down a bit but that he was determined to do as much as he used to.

Also, in that article, Free State football coach Bob Lisher, who played lineman for Dad and served as an assistant coach on his LHS staff, told Bedore, "Coach Freeman is a fighter. He always has been. He's always taken things straight on. Generally, he wins."

The people who knew Dad well certainly believed he could handle Alzheimer's, just like he handled everything else. And he did, for a while, but even Alzheimer's gets the best of its victims at some point, no matter how tough they may be. Bill Freeman was no exception. In the summer of 2012, we decided, as a family, that it was in the best interest of Dad and every-

Jennifer and Bill Freeman, Lifecare Nursing Home, Burlington, Kansas, summer 2014

one else to move him to an assisted living facility. He needed to be where he could have full time care and attention. It had become a matter of safety, and because we loved him, we made the difficult decision to place him in the Life Care Center in Burlington, Kansas.

My grandmother had actually been in the same facility, so we knew it was a good choice. Plus, they had an excellent Alzheimer's unit, and it was only fifteen minutes from Leroy. This is never what anyone wants, and I can't stress that enough. It is a heart-wrenching decision, one you always second guess, and one that you can't possibly imagine until you're faced with it.

I am forever grateful to the staff there. They took very good care of Dad and loved him very much. Dad, on the other hand, did *not* want to be there and pleaded with me every time I went to visit him to take him home. It was excruciating to tell him I couldn't because I wanted, more than anything, for that to be possible. I wished this was all just a bad dream and that I could put him in the car and drive him back home and everything would return to normal. He looked at me with these sad, helpless, puppy dog eyes, and it killed me.

I visited three to four times a week and tried to make the most out of the time we had. It got easier as time wore on and his stubborn streak got worn down. I took an insane amount of pictures every time I visited, which he hated, but I took them anyway. I brought the kids with me as often as possible, which always made his face light up. Vanilla ice cream shakes from Dairy Queen also made his face light up—we enjoyed our fair share of those during his three years at the Life Care Center. He always asked me to bring him a vanilla shake and some fruit, and when I arrived, he would tell me I could have the fruit and he got the shake. He never lost his ornery side.

Dad had lots of visitors. I know many of his former players and people from Leroy made the trek to Burlington often to spend time with him, a testament to how much he was loved. Jeff True, who hunted arrowheads with Dad, was a regular, bringing Dad his latest finds. Even after Dad could no longer remember Jeff's name or connection to him, the language of arrowheads still untied them. During one of the last times he visited, Jeff recalls holding out a special arrowhead to Dad, whose face immediately broke into his beaming grin. He couldn't speak, but he reached out and took the arrowhead from Jeff and rolled it over in his fingers several times. It was as if he knew it was significant, even though he could not remember why.

About a year before he died, sometime in the fall of 2014, Dad fell and broke his hip. He had to be taken to Fredonia Regional Hospital, about fifty miles away, where he remained for almost a month. During that time, we didn't see him, and once he was back at the Life Care Center in Burlington, we saw a noticeable decline begin to occur.

That, in a way, was the beginning of the end. Once confined to a wheelchair, Dad became increasingly irritable, began to put on weight, and gradually lost physical function and his capacity for speech. I think he could still understand what we were saying to him, but most of the time, he would look at us with a blank stare.

He hung in there for another year until November of 2015 when he developed a severe case of pneumonia. He had had a bad cold, but we had no idea it was anything more until I received a call from an ER doctor at the Coffey County Medical Center in Burlington. It was barely after midnight on Black Friday, and I had driven to Kansas City to take advantage of Black Friday deals. The doctor explained that they were unable to reach my mom and that they needed permission to intubate Dad and transport him to St. Francis Hospital in Topeka. He said Dad's blood pressure was dropping and he was afraid he wasn't going to make it. I gave permission and raced to Topeka, fearing the absolute worst.

When we arrived, my worst fears did, in fact, come true. Dad was not going to survive this. He had lost his swallow reflex, so the doctors proposed inserting a feeding tube, but it was left up to us to decide, a wrenching decision to have to make. Without it, he wouldn't be able to eat, but in his weakened condition, it was a risk just to do the procedure. If we opted not to insert the feeding tube, he would eventually starve to death. If we opted to insert the feeding tube, the procedure itself could kill him.

We asked ourselves, "What would Dad want?" Although painful, the answer was clear. He would not have wanted to linger in a non-communicative state, unable to move or function on his own. He had made those wishes known in his living will, but anyone who knew Bill Freeman would've known that those were his wishes. He was far too strong, stubborn, and independent to want to live this way, so we chose to forgo the feeding tube and have Dad moved back to the Life Care Center in Burlington for whatever time he had left.

I walked out of the hospital in Topeka that night feeling nauseated. I felt like a horrible daughter. I wondered if we were cheating Dad. I knew we were honoring his wishes, but I wanted to be selfish. I wanted to do any and everything possible to keep him around a little bit longer. I wasn't ready to let go.

Once he was back in Burlington, they called in a hospice nurse who pointed out that he was "mottling." I had no idea what that meant, but she explained that it referred to the blotchy, bluish-purplish coloring on his knees and feet and that it was a sign that the end was near. In her estimation, Dad probably had six to eight weeks.

I visited Dad every day. He was almost always asleep, but I sat by his side anyway and told him about my day and what the kids were up to, or sometimes, I just sat in silence. It didn't matter. I just wanted to soak up every opportunity to be with him that I could.

As Dad's condition worsened, we notified family, and on Wednesday, December 16, 2015, we all gathered in his room. Dad's sister and her husband, her daughter and her husband, my mom, my brother, my three children, and me—all huddled together in his tiny room. Surprisingly, Dad was awake the entire time, four hours or more. He couldn't speak, but his eyes were open and there were waves of recognition that passed over his face from time to time. He was "there" as much as he could be, and I'd like to think he heard and understood everything we said.

We all took our respective turns to talk to Dad and tell him good-bye. It was truly painful, but nobody wanted to leave. We just lingered on into the night. This was the first time that our family had dealt with anything like this, the first time any of us had experienced the death of someone so close. If I'm being honest and not worrying about being eloquent and articulate, there is no other way to describe that night other than to say it sucked. It was the last time I would see him alive.

Not even two full days later, in the wee hours of the morning on Friday, December 18, one of the nurses called and said she thought it was time—if we wanted to be there, we needed to come now. I got everyone up and we hurried to Burlington, but we didn't make it in time. Dad passed away only moments before we arrived.

I felt like I had been hit with a wrecking ball. I fell to the floor, screaming and sobbing uncontrollably, so much so that they had to put me in a conference room to calm down because I was waking up the other residents. Once I composed myself a bit, the nurses let me go in and spend as much time with Dad as I needed.

It was shocking to see him lying there, so still and cold. I knew he was going to die, but somehow, I was still surprised at the news. I dropped to my knees on the cold, hard floor beside his bed and placed my hands over his. I kept thinking, "Take a breath. Come on," as if I could will him back to life. I just wanted to see his chest rise one more time.

Between sobs, I stroked his hair and patted his cheek. I spoke to him aloud, telling him I loved him and that he was my hero. I thanked him—I would not be where I am today or who I am today without him. He was hard as hell on me at times, and believe me, like any daughter, there were times I could not stand him. We were often like oil and water, but through it all, there was love. He was the calm in my storm, and now he was gone. In that moment, I could not imagine life without him.

Chapter 5

Bill Freeman, the Legend

"We can all be successful and make money, but when we die, that ends. But when you are significant is when you help other people be successful. That lasts many a lifetime."
Lou Holtz

Bill Freeman was not a man who enjoyed the limelight, but several years before his death, I began a crusade to get him the recognition he duly deserved, namely, a spot in the Kansas Sports Hall of Fame. It was not something he would've ever done on his own, but it was a prestigious honor that he had earned, and as his health declined, I became more determined than ever to make it happen while he was still alive.

Dad had received many other accolades through the years. In 1973, he was a Kansas Shrine Bowl Coach and in 1996, was selected to the National Football Foundation College Hall of

Fame. He was inducted to the Emporia State Hall of Fame and the Kansas State High School Activities Association Hall of Fame, and in 2012, Dad received the Kansas Sports Hall of Fame's "Pride of Kansas" award. It is given to coaches and athletes who achieved a lifetime of greatness while maintaining the highest level of integrity influencing the lives of youth.

That is where my quest began. This award is the second highest honor given to a high school coach and is typically considered a stepping stone to an election into the Kansas Sports Hall of Fame, usually the following year. However, Dad was passed over in 2013, much to the disappointment of many who fully anticipated him to be a shoe-in. I was not going to settle for that. Dad deserved to be in the Hall of Fame, so in October of 2013, I decided to do whatever was in my power to make it happen. It would be the most prestigious of all the honors Dad had received, and I saw it as one of the "last things" he had yet to do in his lifetime.

I got busy. I created a Facebook page titled, "Help Get Coach Freeman Inducted into the Kansas Sports Hall of Fame" and began reaching out to former players, coaches, friends, and media on my father's behalf, asking them to write letters to Jordan Poland, the Director of the Kansas Sports Hall of Fame. Poland was tasked with compiling a list of twenty-five nominees and placing their names on a ballot that would go out to the media as well as other contributors and donors around the state. The tremendous response and outpouring of support for my dad's nomination was overwhelming. Many people posted on the Facebook page, ten wrote letters to Poland, and five newspapers ran articles. Clearly, I wasn't the only one who thought Dad deserved to be a Hall of Famer.

All our efforts paid off. The ballots were mailed out in early April of 2014, and Dad was on it, but that was just the first hurdle. Once the ballots went out, it was a nerve-wracking waiting game. Voters had until May 2 to return the ballots, but we were told that the announcement of the Hall of Fame inductees would not be made until late June or early July. I was on pins and needles waiting to hear the news I had hoped and prayed for for many months.

My birthday is at the end of May, and I had been telling everyone that year that all I wanted was for Dad to be voted in to the Hall of Fame. On Thursday, May 29, one day before my birthday, I received an early birthday present when I got a phone call from Jordan Poland with the good news I had been waiting for – Dad was going to be inducted to the Kansas Sports Hall of Fame!

I could barely speak. I hung up the phone and bawled like a baby. I was so emotional. It was truly a dream come true. The ceremony wouldn't occur until October 5 in Wichita, but I couldn't wait to see my dad and deliver the good news. When I told him that he was going to be a Hall of Famer, he flashed his signature Freeman grin. I don't know if he understood what I was saying, but I'd like to believe he did. I'd like to believe it meant as much to him as it did to me.

Obviously, Dad was not able to attend the ceremony in Wichita that Fall, but I took plenty of pictures to show him

Bill's grandchildren at the Hall of Fame induction ceremony, October 2014

afterward. It was a wonderful ceremony and so amazing to see the Hall of Fame Wichita Boat House packed with people celebrating the accomplishments of the inductees. Before each honoree was presented with their plaque, there was a slideshow about his or her life and career highlights. It was a moving tribute and especially emotional for me since Dad was not there to see it himself. My three children accepted the award on Dad's behalf, and we delivered it to him in Burlington the very next day.

Shortly after Dad's death, in the first few months of 2016, I began working on two additional initiatives to honor my father. The first was my personal attempt to raise awareness about the devastating effects of Alzheimer's in hopes that one day, there might be a cure. According to the Alzheimer's Association, five million Americans are living with Alzheimer's, and by 2050, it is projected that the number could rise as high as sixteen million. Every sixty-six seconds, an American is diagnosed with the disease, and since the year 2000, deaths from Alzheimer's have increased by eighty-nine percent. In the state of Kansas alone, it was estimated that in 2017, Alzheimer's affected fifty-two thousand people, and that number is expected to jump to more than sixty-two thousand by the year 2025.

Watching my Dad lose himself to this debilitating disease was painful, a deep, searing pain like nothing I had ever known before. I would not wish it upon anyone else. I felt moved to do something—anything—to try to help others going through the same suffering. I'm not sure where my idea came from, but I wanted to do something not only to carry on Dad's legacy, but also to support awareness and research for this disease that impacts so many lives. I reached out to Kansas State Representative Peggy Mast, an Emporia Republican and Speaker Pro Tem of the Kansas House. I told her about my dad and asked if she would consider drafting a bill to create a special Kansas license plate to draw attention to Alzheimer's.

She immediately agreed to my request and suggested that I contact as many media outlets as possible to share my story and gain support for the bill. I also reached out once again via Facebook to ask people to write letters in favor of the legislation.

It quickly took on a life of its own, and by mid-January of 2016, House Bill 2473 was introduced and referred on to the House Transportation Committee, where I was given the opportunity to present my proposal. I explained to the committee what it was like to see this disease rob my father of his memory, to see him go from being a strong, independent father, husband, friend, and grandpa to a man who couldn't remember where he parked the car or what time it was or where we lived.

My hopes that the bill would quickly be signed into law were dashed when the bill stalled because it lacked sponsorship. I didn't know where to turn or what to do next, but about a month later, while attending an Alzheimer's forum at the University of Kansas Clinical Research Center with Kansas Senator Jerry Moran, I raised my hand and shared the story of my father. I explained how the bill had languished and that I didn't know what, if anything, I could do to help move it along.

A gentleman in the audience immediately spoke up, offering to sponsor the bill. I was speechless. I hadn't known I needed a sponsor to begin with and wasn't even exactly sure what that meant, but he said he would take care of it. The bill unanimously passed in the House a few days later and went before the Senate in March, where it also passed unanimously. On May 11, 2016, Governor Sam Brownback signed it into law.

The other initiative I worked on in the early part of 2016 was not as successful, but certainly worth a try. I petitioned the Lawrence School Board, asking that either the stadium or the football field at Lawrence High School be named in honor of Bill Freeman. With former players, coaches, and friends in attendance, I presented my proposal at the school board meeting on February 8, 2016. I saw the naming effort as a way to pay tribute to the impact that Dad had on the school. He turned the football program around and created not only a winning culture, but an inclusive culture.

I acknowledged that there had been other great coaches in the history of Lawrence football, equally deserving, but of course, for me, this was personal, and I felt that Dad deserved this honor. Ultimately, the board agreed with a Lawrence High committee who recommended that the field and stadium remain nameless. The committee believed that the practice of naming any one athletic facility after an individual was not in its best interest and not something it should begin doing. Given the storied athletic history of the school, they felt like it would be impossible and unfair to honor one person over others.

While disappointed, I completely understood and was, in no way, trying to overshadow the accomplishments of other great

and well-deserving Lawrence High coaches. The committee suggested that coaching legends could be recognized in other ways, such as public markers, statues, plaques, etc. That would certainly

Jennifer at the Hall of Fame, Wichita, 2015

accomplish my goal, which is to simply honor the sacrifices all coaches and teachers make for their players and students.

As if 2016 wasn't busy enough, one more accolade was bestowed upon Dad posthumously. In 2015, the Greater Kansas City Football Coaches Association instituted its own Hall of Fame with a permanent display at Arrowhead Stadium, home of the Kansas City Chiefs. The Hall of Fame honors pioneer coaches, coaches, players, and associates who have contributed to the hundred-year Kansas City high school football tradition.

Dad was inducted into its second class in the summer of 2016 as a "Pioneer" Coach, alongside other Kansas City area coaching legends.

Legend. Although my dad would never have used this word to describe himself, I certainly think of him that way. I am so proud of him, not just of him as a coach, but of him as a person – a person who was kind-hearted, tough, strong, and hard-working. He was a winner who knew how to have fun and enjoy life, love, and laughter. His former players and students who now teach and coach aspire to be just like him because the legacy he passed on was that of kindness and care for others. If that's not a legend, I don't know what is.

Chapter 6

The Legend Lives On

"A good coach will make his players see what they can be rather than what they are."
Ara Parseghian

If you ask people for one word to describe Bill Freeman, you'll hear things like tough, demanding, hard-working, stubborn, competitive, proud, but you'll also be told he was humble, loving, caring, and loyal. All of these words aptly describe my dad as he was, in fact, all of these things. As I talked with his former players and colleagues while writing this book, I was struck by how many of them described Dad in just such a way. It also surprised and amazed me how

Bill during a Lawrence High School football game, circa 1984

many of them attribute their own successes on and off the field to my father. They credit him with their prosperous careers and happy lives, acknowledging that they are who they are because of his influence.

In a written question and answer interview for this book, Keith Cobb responded, "I would say that how he taught his players to be *men* on and off the field is something that cannot be replaced. I often think back to my days with LHS football, what he taught me about how to compete, how to deal with being in a tough situation, how to deal with that situation and work your way in order to come out on top. This has carried with me as a person in how I deal with my family, my job and everyday life. He had many wins, state championships, league titles, was elected to the Kansas Coaches Hall of Fame, but I know what he has meant to me and my life beyond my high school years of LHS football. This will never be replaced."

Many shared with me that they constantly ask themselves in difficult situations, "What would Coach Freeman do?" They hear his squeaky voice echoing in the back of their minds while they, themselves, are coaching, even if it's just little league. In a beautiful testament to my father's impact, Scott Stidham wrote, "Now that I'm a coach myself, I realize that his greatest achievement is the difference he made in so many young men's lives. The men who played for Coach have not only gone on to success on the athletic field, but also in life. The husbands, fathers, and successful professionals all over the world are his greatest achievement."

While I was trying to drum up support for Dad's nomination into the Kansas Sports Hall of Fame, former player Mike Hughes wrote to the nominating committee, and in the following excerpt, truly spoke to the depth and breadth of Dad's impact on his life. "Today, I like to tell the kids I coach that the harder you work, the easier it gets. That comes from Coach. Twenty-three years later, I can still feel Coach's influence in my teaching. Because of Coach Freeman, I still believe you are a product of yourself: in sports, in school, and in life. The harder you work, the easier it gets – that doesn't stop when you leave the field, court, track, mat, or rink. Coach instilled that in many of his student-athletes, and his success both on and off the field proves that it works. He instilled in me many things as an athlete, but I have found that I learned a far greater deal about life."

"Thanks to the influence of teaching, mentoring, and growth from Coach Freeman," said former LHS football player Kent Thomas, "I coached girls high school basketball for several years and – not knowing anything about anything when I started – leaned on the foundation of how to build a program, teach, communicate, motivate and quietly/humbly lead learned from Coach."

In these ways, my dad's legacy continues to live on in the hearts and minds of those who knew and loved him, and in some ways, in the hearts and minds of those who didn't know him. Teachers and coaches at Lawrence High say they often hear younger coaches or even parents shouting "Freemanims" from the sidelines that they must have picked up from their parents or

mentors who knew my dad. It is gratifying to know that he touched so many lives beyond just our family and comforting to believe that every time someone remembers him or quotes him, a little piece of him remains and gets passed on.

Coach Ron Commons, Scott Stidham and Coach Bill Freeman, Lawrence High School football game, 1988

Days after Dad's death in 2015, the *Miami County Republic* published an article by Garett McCullough, recapping many of Dad's accomplishments. In addition to his career highlights, McCullough writes about the qualities that made Dad not only a fine coach, but an exemplary human being. He references an article written a year earlier in which former Osawatomie tight end and safety from the 1974 championship team, Ike Brady, was quoted. Ike recalled a situation that captures the kind of man Bill Freeman was beyond football.

Ike was out of town in the early nineties when he received a phone call that his brother had been admitted to the hospital. When he arrived a few days later, he found only two people in the room—his brother and my dad. Nearly twenty years after leaving Osawatomie for Lawrence High School, Dad was there to show his support and pray for his recovery.

"That to me said a lot about the man," Ike said in the article. "There was nobody else there besides Freeman. Other people had visited but had already left. Freeman read about it in the paper. It was not a positive situation. It was a tragic situation that involved some things that weren't very pleasant. He knew my brother and knew him when he was a little kid. He was there for him." That kind of experience is not unique to Ike Brady. It was how my dad lived his life and how he cared for others, always above and beyond what might be expected. He believed that people were worth it and that everyone deserved respect.

When asked, "What is Bill Freeman's greatest legacy?" former coaching colleague and Lawrence Athletic Director Ron Commons put it perfectly. He said, "Bill's greatest legacy is that *everyone* can be successful. You can be whatever it is you want to be."

Chris King said what he learned from my dad is this, "Be dedicated to what you are doing. Never be satisfied. Strive every day to perform better than you did before. Be a student of the game or whatever you are doing in life. Strive for excellence and you will be successful."

I have to agree with Ron and Chris that the greatest legacy Dad leaves behind in a world too often scarred by misperception and prejudice is that *everyone* can do or be whatever they desire. It is within each of us to determine our path, put in the hard work, and go for our goals.

I am as biased as I can be when it comes to my father. Clearly, I worshipped the ground he walked on my entire life and have felt the emptiness of his absence since his death almost three years ago. In many ways, this book is my story of my dad, but in other ways, it is the story of so many people whose lives have been changed because they knew him. I wish I were able to share all the wonderful things others have said to honor my father's memory in this book, but obviously, it would be impossible to print them all. I felt like it was important to share at least a few of the stories and memories as tributes to a man who will not soon be forgotten. I can only hope that during his life on earth, he knew how much he was loved and cherished, but if not, maybe in some way, he will know now.

Bill Freeman was far too humble and unassuming to have thought of himself as anyone special. He would absolutely cringe at the notion that he is a legend, but clearly, I am not the only one who sees him that way. He put everyone else before himself, before winning a football game or track meet, before money or material possessions. Lives have been forever changed because of Bill Freeman, and that is a legacy that will live on forever.

Kansas State Football championship, Memorial Stadium, Lawrence, 1984

Additional Tributes

"Coach was a great man with a loving heart. He loved his family. He cared deeply about making his players better people as well as better athletes. To me, he is a legendary figure in my life and the thousands of people he either coached, taught, or had dealings with in business. He was a legend who I miss and think about every day."

-Bob Lisher, former player and coaching colleague

"I'm a better person—husband, father, grandfather, teacher, friend—today because of his influence on me."

-Chuck Holley, former Lawrence High coach

"I'll paraphrase Jackie Robinson's tombstone: 'Life is meaningless except how it impacts others.' If you judge Coach Freeman's life by that criteria, he was one of the best, considering all the people he impacted."

-Chip Budde, former LHS and KU lineman

"He instilled a foundation of believing in yourself. Coming off a 1-6 campaign after my sophomore year, I was a junior when Bill Freeman took over. His discipline was sorely needed, yeah we only won three games my junior year. He didn't quit and neither did we. My senior year, LHS finally posted a winning football season, and of course after that, the program took off. It was during my first year with Coach that I decided I wanted to go into sportscasting. I saw how he made a difference and wanted to be in a position to share with viewers stories of coaches who had influence. Truly a great man who had a tremendous heart. My younger cousins would go on to play for him. Colemans are proud to have played for Coach. Gary would become an All-American under him, me a Shrine Bowl All-Star because of what he instilled in us."

-Michael Coleman, former player and sportscaster

"What Coach was, was a farmer. The seed he planted in our lives...the seeds would last a lifetime. Some of his sayings have been words of inspiration to carry me. Coach said, 'Boys, for sure the sun will rise tomorrow.' He meant regardless of whether we win or lose, give your best. If we win, the sun will rise. If we lose, the sun will rise. They were short and sweet and had a profound impact on my life."

-Steve Barbee, former LHS running back

"Coach Freeman was an amazing man who touched the lives of so many, including myself. He was high on principle and doing things the right way."

-Tom Williams, 1989 state pole vault champion

"What a good mentor he was to his coaching staff and the kids he had an opportunity to coach, whether football players or track athletes. As far as I was concerned, Bill was that impact person in all our lives."

-Ron Commons, former coach and athletic director at LHS

"He [Bill Freeman], next to my father, is one of the most influential men in my life...I still carry with me some of the work ethic, integrity, self-respect, and humility that Coach taught me. As much as I hated that man when I just wanted practice to be over and he would yell, 'One more play!' I think I came as close to loving him as a non-family member as I could get."

-Geoff Lutz, former LHS player

"In those short few months, I learned many life lessons that I have applied throughout the years whether at work building a better team or coaching our kids' youth basketball or baseball teams. It was always about fundamentals and effort. Through the years, I often thought of Coach and shared stories with my kids and friends. In his passing, I find myself reflecting on those life lessons learned and trying in some small way to keep his legacy alive."

-Brian Torres, former player

"One of the underlying themes behind the love that so many of us have for Coach Freeman is that he inspired each of us to do our best."

-Jason Young, former track athlete

"And as sports writers—whether it was Quake, or G.B., Rick Dean, Kurt Caywood, or anyone else—we loved him. We marveled at how this modest man, who was as down-to-earth as the tree roots in his treasured pecan grove, was such an accomplished teacher, coach, banker, rancher, farmer, father, and grandfather."

-Kevin Haskin, former *Topeka Capital Journal* sportswriter

Acknowledgements

My heart is overflowing with gratitude for the many people who were a part of this book, either directly or indirectly. I could not have done it without them. This book was truly a labor of love and a dream come true.

First and foremost, thank you to my family who love and support me every single day.

This book would not have been possible without the contributions of so many of Dad's former players and fellow coaches. Thank you, Lynn Dickey, for your willingness to be interviewed and also for your beautiful words about Dad in the foreword of this book.

Thank you also to former players, Jeff Wright and Cam Miller, for the time you took and the stories you shared in phone interviews for this book. To some of Dad's coaching colleagues, Ron Commons, Don Gardner, and Bob Whitehead—many thanks to you for the generosity of your time and insights offered in phone interviews as well.

The written responses and reflections provided by former players and coaches, Bob Lisher, Scott Stidham, Chris King, Ron Oelschlager, and Keith Cobb were invaluable in putting together the many anecdotes about Dad. I appreciate your willingness to share so many of your memories in writing. There are many other tributes in this book from former players and coaches that were reprinted from various newspaper articles about my dad – thank you to each and every person whose beautiful words and memories of my father are captured in these pages.

I also want to thank Brian Torres, Geoff Lutz, and Mike Hughes for allowing us to reprint portions of letters and emails they had written several years ago remembering Dad.

A special thanks to Jeff True, whose phone interview provided a unique perspective of Dad that only he could offer—thank you, Jeff.

Thank you to the various sports journalists who covered Kansas high school football over the years and whose numerous articles about my father provided many important details not only about his coaching career, but his personal life, death, and legacy as well. A special thanks to Gary Bedore, Kurt Caywood, and Garett McCollough, as well as to the *Lawrence Journal World*, the *Topeka Capital Journal*, and the *Miami County Republic* who graciously gave us permission to reprint excerpts of various newspaper articles. A heartfelt posthumous thank-you to sportswriter Allen Quakenbush.

Finally, a very special, heartfelt thank you to all the people of Leroy, Kansas whose continued love and support for our family over the years still buoys me up and helps keep the memory of my dad alive.

About the Authors

Jennifer Freeman, proud mother of three adult children, lives in Leroy, Kansas and still loves high school football. She is passionate about raising awareness to help find a cure for Alzheimer's and has established the Bill Freeman Foundation in honor of her late father. She spends her spare time with friends and family and loves to travel anywhere there is a beach, but Hawaii is her favorite. Jennifer is available for book signings and presentations. She can be reached at jennylew18@yahoo.com.

Tina Wendling is a ghostwriter, editor, and book coach who lives in Kansas City, Missouri with her husband and two teenage sons. Her passion is helping other people tell their stories by putting words to their ideas. She is honored to be a part of this project and has been inspired by the legacy of Bill Freeman and all the wonderful former players and coaches she had the privilege to interview. If you have a book idea or a project already underway that needs some help, Tina can be reached at tina@truelifelegacies.com.

Made in the USA
Columbia, SC
11 November 2018